SEP   2013

Weight Management

YOUNG ADULT'S GUIDE TO THE SCIENCE OF HEALTH

Allergies & Asthma

Contraception & Pregnancy

Coping with Moods

Dental Care

Drug- & Alcohol-Related Health Issues

Fitness & Nutrition

Growth & Development

Health Implications of Cosmetic Surgery,
Makeovers, & Body Alterations

Healthy Skin

Managing Stress

Sexually Transmitted Infections

Sleep Deprivation & Its Consequences

Smoking-Related Health Issues

Suicide & Self-Destructive Behaviors

Weight Management

Young Adult's Guide to the Science of Health

Weight Management

Elizabeth Bauchner

MASON CREST

Mason Crest
450 Parkway Drive, Suite D
Broomall, PA 19008
www.masoncrest.com

Printed in the Hashemite Kingdom of Jordan.

First printing
9 8 7 6 5 4 3 2 1

Series ISBN: 978-1-4222-2803-6
ISBN: 978-1-4222-2818-0
ebook ISBN: 978-1-4222-9014-9

The Library of Congress has cataloged the
        hardcopy format(s) as follows:

        Library of Congress Cataloging-in-Publication Data

Bauchner, Elizabeth.
  Weight management / Elizabeth Bauchner.
      pages cm – (Young adult's guide to the science of health)
  Includes index.
  Audience: 7-8.
  Audience: Grade 7 to 8.
  ISBN 978-1-4222-2818-0 (hardcover) – ISBN 978-1-4222-2803-6 (series) – ISBN 978-1-4222-9014-9
(ebook)
  1. Weight loss–Juvenile literature. I. Title.
  RM222.2.B3856 2014
  613.2'5–dc23
                        2013006394

Designed and produced by Vestal Creative Services.
www.vestalcreative.com

Contents

Introduction

by Dr. Sara Forman

You're not a little kid anymore. When you look in the mirror, you probably see a new person, someone who's taller, bigger, with a face that's starting to look more like an adult's than a child's. And the changes you're experiencing on the inside may be even more intense than the ones you see in the mirror. Your emotions are changing, your attitudes are changing, and even the way you think is changing. Your friends are probably more important to you than they used to be, and you no longer expect your parents to make all your decisions for you. You may be asking more questions and posing more challenges to the adults in your life. You might experiment with new identities—new ways of dressing, hairstyles, ways of talking—as you try to determine just who you really are. Your body is maturing sexually, giving you a whole new set of confusing and exciting feelings. Sorting out what is right and wrong for you may seem overwhelming.

Growth and development during adolescence is a multifaceted process involving every aspect of your being. It all happens so fast that it can be confusing and distressing. But this stage of your life is entirely normal. Every adult in your life made it through adolescence—and you will too.

But what exactly is adolescence? According to the American Heritage Dictionary, adolescence is "the period of physical and psychological development from the onset of puberty to adulthood." What does this really mean?

In essence, adolescence is the time in our lives when the needs of childhood give way to the responsibilities of adulthood. According to psychologist Erik Erikson, these years are a time of separation and individuation. In other words, you are separating from your parents, becoming an individual in your own right. These are the years when you begin to make decisions on your own. You are becoming more self-reliant and less dependent on family members.

When medical professionals look at what's happening physically—what they refer to as the biological model—they define the teen years as a period of hormonal transformation toward sexual maturity, as well as a time of peak growth, second only to the growth during the months of infancy. This physical transformation from childhood to adulthood takes place under the influence of society's norms and social pressures; at the same time your body is changing, the people around you are expecting new things from you. This is what makes adolescence such a unique and challenging time.

Being a teenager in North America today is exciting yet stressful. For those who work with teens, whether by parenting them, educating them, or providing services to them, adolescence can be challenging as well. Youth are struggling with many messages from society and the media about how they should behave and who they should be. "Am I normal?" and "How do I fit in?" are often questions with which teens wrestle. They are facing decisions about their health such as how to take care of their bodies, whether to use drugs and alcohol, or whether to have sex.

This series of books on adolescents' health issues provides teens, their parents, their teachers, and all those who work with them accurate information and the tools to keep them safe and healthy. The topics include information about:

- normal growth
- social pressures
- emotional issues
- specific diseases to which adolescents are prone
- stressors facing youth today
- sexuality

The series is a dynamic set of books, which can be shared by youth and the adults who care for them. By providing this information to educate in these areas, these books will help build a foundation for readers so they can begin to work on improving the health and well-being of youth today.

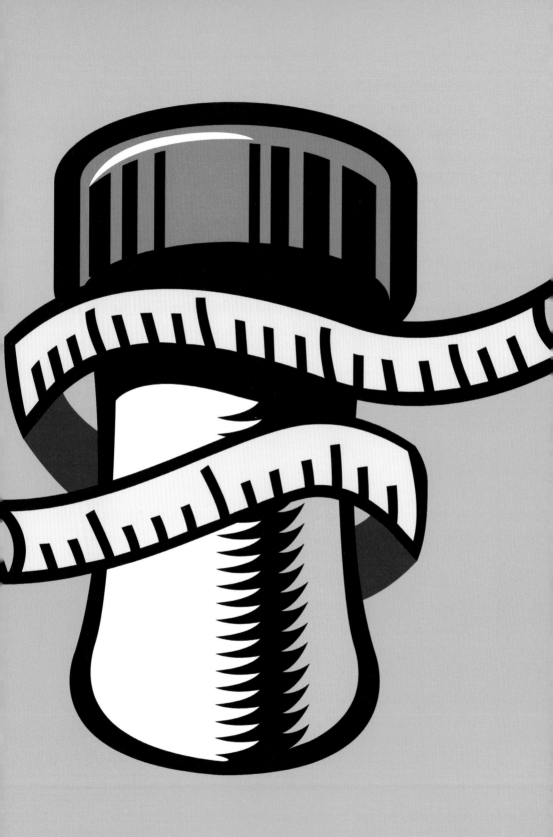

1

Do I Need to Lose Weight?

Fifteen-year-old Jenny has an active social life with several friends. They like to study together, go to the movies, and have sleepovers. At one sleepover, as Jenny and her friends tried on different outfits and jewelry in front of her mother's full-length mirror, Jenny realizes for the first time that she's getting quite a bit larger than her friends.

At first, Jenny's weight startles her. How did she gain so much weight so fast? She didn't think she was overweight in middle school. In fact, she isn't all that sure she really is overweight now, or if she should go on a diet. All she knows is that she's larger

than her friends—and she wants to do something about it. After speaking with her mother about her concerns, she agrees to go to the doctor for some advice on healthy weight management.

Could You Be Overweight?

According to the Centers for Disease Control and Prevention (CDC), the percentage of American children and teens who are defined as overweight has more than tripled since the early 1970s. About 17 percent of children and adolescents are now overweight.

Being overweight refers to an excess of body weight, but not necessarily body fat. A muscular person may be considered "overweight" because muscle weighs more than fat. Obesity, however, means an excessively high proportion of body fat. For teens who suspect that they have a weight problem, it's good to ask a parent or caregiver to schedule an appointment with a health care provider. She will discuss dietary needs and lifestyle, as well as any changes a person may need to make.

One of the first things a health care provider is likely to do is to check the person's body mass index (BMI). BMI is a number that shows body weight adjusted for height. It can be calculated with simple math using inches and pounds, or meters and kilograms. For adults over twenty years old, BMI falls into one of these categories: underweight, normal, overweight, or obese. For children and teens, health care professionals use a slightly different method of calculating BMI, called BMI-for-age, that takes into account age and gender to determine if the person is underweight, overweight, or at risk for becoming overweight.

It's important for teens to talk with their health care providers about any weight concerns they may have, and not to compare themselves with their friends as Jenny did—but that can

Physical appearance is often more important to teens than to younger individuals, and comparing themselves to one another is common. Before deciding you're overweight, be sure to consult your medical practitioner.

be difficult at times, especially for teens. Each person's development is unique. Taller people may weigh more than shorter people and still fall within a healthy weight range. Also, teens need some body fat to remain healthy; the problem is having an excess of body fat. Each person's health care provider will be able to help her determine if she needs to lose weight, how much she should lose, and how to go about it.

Do I Need to Lose Weight?

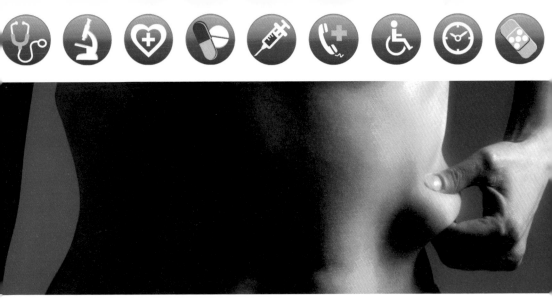

How Do I Know If I Need to Lose Weight?

Not everyone is meant to be ultra-thin or look like the models in magazines, or even to look like anyone else in particular except himself. People come in all shapes and sizes. A person's height, body type, and level of exercise will all determine what his OPTIMUM weight should be. Each person's health care provider can help him figure this out by checking BMI and discussing diet and lifestyles.

What someone weighs is actually the result of several factors: how much and what kinds of food a person eats, whether or not her lifestyle includes regular physical activity, whether she uses food to respond to stress and other situations in her life, her physiologic and GENETIC makeup, her age, and her health status. Successful weight loss and weight management takes all these factors into consideration.

A word of caution: extraordinary concern or obsession for thinness leads some teens to eating disorders such as bulimia nervosa (overeating and then vomiting) or anorexia nervosa (dieting to literal starvation). It is important for people to follow their health care providers' advice for healthy weight man-

agement to avoid an eating disorder. We will discuss more on eating disorders in a later chapter.

Why Should Overweight People Lose Weight?

When someone's health care provider determines that he is overweight or obese, he is at increased risk for more health problems such as high blood pressure, TYPE II DIABETES, and heart disease (explained more thoroughly in chapter 3). In general, the higher a person's BMI, the higher their health risks, and the risks increase the larger their waist size becomes. Health care providers can give people advice about their overall health risks and the weight loss options that are best for them.

People decide to lose weight for many reasons: to be healthier, to feel better and have more energy, and to look better. What-

WHAT TO LOOK FOR IN A HEALTH CARE PROVIDER

Some doctors now recommend that teens find health care providers who specialize in adolescent medicine. Sometimes, teens simply find that they have outgrown their pediatrician. Regardless of whether teens see a pediatrician or other doctor, however, they should feel comfortable speaking with their doctor about all kinds of health issues, including diet and weight loss, exercise, puberty, and even substance abuse and sexuality issues. Find a doctor willing to talk with teens, not just with parents, and ask about any privacy issues that may concern teens.

STEPS TO FINDING OUT WHAT A HEALTHY WEIGHT IS FOR YOU

First, see a doctor or health care professional who will check your BMI for your gender and age. Don't judge yourself by how much your friends or relatives weigh. Your level of activity, your height, and other factors contribute to what your ideal body weight should be. A health care professional is the best person to help you figure this out.

ever their reasons for wanting to lose weight, successful weight loss and healthy weight management depends on setting sensible goals and expectations. People are much more likely to lose weight and to keep it off if they take it gradually and not try to do too much at once. Health experts recommend weight loss of about one-half to two pounds per week. Very obese people can lose more weight under a doctor's guidance.

Jenny's doctor helped her determine that she was in fact about twenty pounds overweight. He recommended that the first thing she do was to start exercising more. Six months after her first checkup, Jenny was incorporating physical activity into her daily routine, such as walking to school instead of taking the bus. She also joined a gym so she could swim in the pool a couple of times per week, and she began riding her bike regularly.

Do I Need to Lose Weight?

Weight Management

Like many other teenagers, Jenny found that exercise helped her maintain her weight, and eating a well-balanced diet helped her to lose weight. Her doctor told her that because she is still growing, she needs to eat a variety of foods, but to cut down on sweets and fats. Jenny's doctor also told her to avoid "fad" diets like the Atkins diet and "crash" diets that advocate losing a lot of weight quickly. In general, temporary diets don't work because eventually the person goes back to their old eating habits and regains most or all of the weight they lost. (We will cover dieting more in chapter 4.)

The hardest part for Jenny was changing her eating habits. She doesn't mind and even enjoys getting more exercise, but she's found it challenging to change her diet by cutting back on candy and popcorn, and adding in more fresh fruits and vegetables. However, Jenny feels better than ever; just by altering her eating habits and getting more exercise, she lost almost twenty pounds in six months.

Healthy Eating: What It Means

Several years ago, the United States Food and Drug Administration (FDA) developed the Food Guide Pyramid to help guide North Americans toward making healthier food choices. In 2011, the FDA created MyPlate. As you can see on page 21, the FDA recommends that each day we eat servings of grains, fruit, vegetables, protein, and milk or dairy products.

Following a diet according to MyPlate helps us meet the nutritional requirements of nutrients, vitamins, and minerals we need daily, as well as the Calories and fats we need every day—yes, Calories and fats—without going overboard. A serving size is generally a modest proportion of the food being served. For example, a serving of protein is about the size of a deck of cards, not a sixteen-ounce steak. Although we need a certain amount

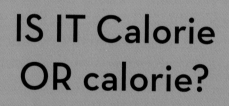

IS IT Calorie OR calorie?

Even if you haven't spent much time learning about food and proper nutrition, you probably have heard the term calorie. But, sometimes it's Calorie. Which is correct? They both are! It just depends on what you're discussing. We measure the amount of energy in a food by a unit called a large, or kilogram, calorie—Calorie with an uppercase "C." Because scientists need to measure small amounts of heat, they use the small calorie unit—yes, that's calorie with a lowercase "c." A calorie with a lowercase "c" refers to the amount of heat it takes to raise the temperature of one gram of water one degree Celsius; a Calorie contains 1000 of these calories.

of fats in our daily diets to help us digest some important vitamins and minerals, fat is high in Calories—and eating too many Calories is what makes us pack on the pounds.

For people who want to lose weight, it's still important to eat a balanced diet. That's why following the MyPlate guidelines can help us achieve a healthy weight.

Quick and Healthy Snacks

Need a quick snack for between classes or after school? Forget vending machines. Pack an apple or banana into your book bag in the morning, or a half of a sandwich, or a bag of pretzels and unbuttered popcorn. Carrot sticks, applesauce, and yogurt also make quick, healthy snacks. Low-fat granola bars or a bowl of

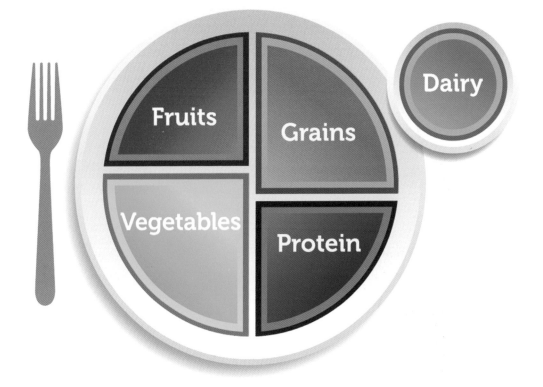

MyPlate provides a guideline for a balanced diet. Find out more at www.choosemyplate.gov.

Fruit and vegetables are healthy snacks.

Weight Management

healthy cereal are quick, after-school or bedtime snacks. Also, carry a water bottle in your bag. Soda is one of the worst foods to consume because of the high number of Calories and sugars.

Losing Weight, Staying Healthy

Whether someone needs to shed just a few pounds or more than two hundred, with the dietary guidelines outlined in My-Plate and recommended by most health experts, DIETITIANS, and NUTRITIONISTS, all people can reach a healthy weight that is right for them. The key points to remember are that it takes time to lose weight in a healthy manner, and a life-long commitment to changing lifestyle habits is necessary to remain healthy for years to come.

2

How Does the
Body Lose Weight?

When Jenny incorporated physical activity into her daily routine, it helped her to get fit, and it will help her to maintain her body weight at the level that is healthy for her. When she changed her diet to include more fresh fruits and vegetables, and less sweets and fats, she lost weight. Her doctor did not recommend that she meticulously count her Calories. He did, however, recommend that she become more aware of how much and what kinds of foods she eats and how she can make healthier food choices.

In this chapter, we'll take a look at what, exactly, Calories are and how our bodies gain and lose weight.

Fats and Calories

So what are fats? Fats, or lipids, are nutrients in foods that our bodies need to build nerve tissues and hormones. Our bodies also use fat as fuel. If a person's body doesn't use the Calories she's eaten as fuel or building blocks, the Calories get converted into fat—and the fat gets stored by the body in fat cells. Over time, these stored up fats can make people overweight. Calories sometimes get a bad rap, but eating a certain amount of Calories per day is crucial for maintaining good health and to help our bodies function properly.

Not All Fats Are Created Equally

Many teens think they need to give up fats in order to lose weight, when in fact fats are necessary for a healthy diet. Teens especially need fats in their diets during their last big growth spurt between the ages of fifteen and eighteen.

All types of fat have the same amount of Calories, but some fats are more harmful than others. Health experts believe that

A Calorie is a unit of energy that measures how much energy food provides to our bodies. Calories come from carbohydrates (various sugars), proteins, and fats. A gram each of carbohydrate or protein contains 4 Calories. A gram of fat contains 9 Calories—more than twice the amount of the other two. It's important to read food labels for this reason. A serving size of food that's higher in proteins or carbohydrates will enable people to feel full while eating fewer Calories—which means they're less apt to accumulate fat. However, too many Calories from carbohydrates and proteins can also make you fat.

Teens often eat fast foods, which are high in fats and Calories.

How Does the Body Lose Weight?

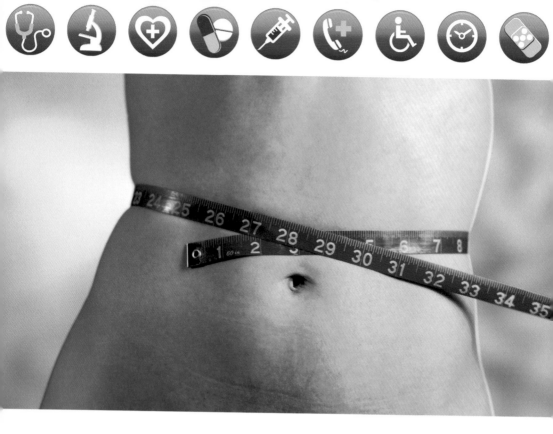

the most dangerous fats are saturated fat and trans fat. Both of these fats can increase a person's risk of heart disease, which means that the arteries pumping blood to and from the heart can become clogged and lead to heart attacks.

Unsaturated fats, while still high in Calories, are much less harmful to our bodies than saturated fats. Unsaturated fats can be polyunsaturated or monounsaturated. Unsaturated fats are liquid at room temperature, such as many vegetable oils, but they are also found in fish, fish oil, nuts, and avocados.

Saturated fats are solid at room temperature and are found in foods like butter, shortening, and the fat on meat. Saturated fats come mostly from animal products, but some tropical oils such as palm kernel oil and coconut oil also contain saturated fat. Trans-fat, which many health experts now believe to be even more dangerous than saturated fat, is found in whole dairy and meat products; however, the most common sources of trans-fat are hydrogenated and partially hydrogenated vegetable oils.

KNOW WHERE YOUR FATS COME FROM

SATURATED FAT: Saturated fat is found mostly in foods from animals and some plants.

   FOODS FROM ANIMALS: beef, beef fat, veal, lamb, pork, lard, poultry fat, butter, cream, milk, cheeses, and other dairy products made from whole milk.

   FOODS FROM PLANTS: coconut oil, palm oil and palm kernel oil (often called tropical oils), and cocoa butter.

UNSATURATED FAT: Polyunsaturated and monounsaturated fats are the two unsaturated fats.

POLYUNSATURATED FAT: safflower, sesame, and sunflower seeds, corn and soybeans, many nuts and seeds, and their oils.

MONOUNSATURATED FAT: canola, olive, and peanut oils, and avocados.

HYDROGENATED FAT: During food processing, fats may undergo a chemical process called hydrogenation. This is common in margarine and shortening.

TRANS-FAT: Trans-fat is found in small amounts in various animal products such as beef, pork, lamb, and the butterfat in butter and milk, and is also formed during the process of hydrogenation. Trans-fat is used in margarine, shortening, and cooking oils, and found in commercially prepared doughnuts, packaged baked goods, cookies, crackers, and potato chips.

Hydrogenation is a process that transforms liquid oils into solid form by adding hydrogen. It is commonly used in products like margarine, packaged baked goods, cookies, crackers, and potato chips because it helps keep the foods fresher longer on store shelves. Their trans-fat content makes these foods an unhealthy snacking choice.

Some Fat Is Necessary

Some fats are necessary for proper growth and good health. For example, fats are necessary for absorbing vitamins A, D, E, and K. These are known as fat-soluble vitamins, which means our bodies will only absorb them if we have fat in our diets.

Teens are still growing and will continue to grow until they are about eighteen years old. Fat is necessary for a developing body. The American Heart Association recommends that people get as much of their daily fat intake as possible from unsaturated fats and to limit their intake of saturated and trans-fat. The U.S. Dietary Guidelines recommend that people get their total daily intake of fat from no more than 30 percent of their daily caloric intake, and the American Heart Association recommends limiting our consumption of saturated and trans-fat to no more than 10 percent of our fat intake.

Sound confusing? It's not, really. It's quite easy learning how to plan meals and snacks that are low in fat and healthy. It's also quite easy to learn to read food labels to decide whether a certain food is a good choice to eat and how much (or how little) of a certain food to eat.

What the Labels Say, and What They Mean

Reading food labels can be tricky. Even though they clearly list how many Calories are in a serving, some math is involved if

Nutrition Facts

Serving Size 1 cup (240mL)
Servings Per Container about 2

Amount Per Serving

Calories 190   Calories from Fat 80

	% Daily Value*
Total Fat 9g	14%
Saturated Fat 1.5g	8%
Trans Fat 0g	
Cholesterol 25mg	8%
Sodium 850mg	35%
Total Carbohydrate 20g	7%
Dietary Fiber 3g	12%
Sugars 4g	
Protein 8g	

Vitamin A 40%	•	Vitamin C 0%
Calcium 2%	•	Iron 4%

* Percent Daily Values are based on a 2,000
calorie diet. Your daily values may be higher
or lower depending on your calorie needs:

	Calories:	2,000	2,500
Total Fat	Less than	65g	80g
Sat Fat	Less than	20g	25g
Cholesterol	Less than	300mg	300mg
Sodium	Less than	2,400mg	2,400mg
Total Carbohydrate	Less than	300g	375g
Dietary			30g

people end up eating more than one serving. For example, a bag of cookies may list three cookies as a serving, but if a person eats six cookies, she will have to double the number of Calories in one serving to find out how many she really consumed.

In order for someone to figure out their caloric intake, the first thing he needs to do when reading food labels is to look at the serving size. Then, see how many Calories are in one serving, and multiply the number of Calories by the number of servings he is going to eat. It's surprising how small some of the serving sizes are on some of our favorite foods!

As for fats, labels can say many things: low-fat, reduced fat, light (or lite), and fat-free are common labels on the front of the package. Here is where it's most important to know how to read the food label to understand how much fat is really in a particular food.

The U.S. government has strict guidelines for the use of the labels fat-free and low-fat. Fat-free foods can contain no more than 0.5 grams of fat. Low-fat foods may contain 3 grams of fat or less. Foods advertised as reduced fat and lite are a little trickier because they may still be high in fat. In order for a food to be labeled "lite" it must contain 50 percent less fat or one-third less Calories than the original version. Foods labeled reduced-fat must contain 25 percent less fat than the original. However, if the original version was a very high-fat food, the reduced fat or lite version may still be high in fat, making it a poor snacking choice. What's more, low-fat foods often add more sugar to make them taste better—so they may be low in fat, but still high in Calories (and our body turns Calories into fat).

Furthermore, labels do not tell it all. It is important to know how many Calories you get from fat, but the percentage isn't always listed on the label. It is, however, easy to calculate. In order to figure the percentage of fat from Calories, divide the number

Food labels on cheese provide information on calories, fat content, and other nutritional information.

How Does the Body Lose Weight?

People often snack on junk food while they watch television.

of Calories from fat by the number of total Calories and multiply by 100.

For example, if a 300-Calorie food has 60 Calories from fat, you divide 60 by 300 (which equals .2) and multiply it by 100, which equals 20, so 20 percent of its Calories come from fat.

Remember, the dietary guidelines are that no more than 30 percent of a person's Calories should come from fat, and no more than 10 percent of those Calories should come from saturated or trans-fat. For someone who wants to lose weight, knowing

Weight Management

how much fat she normally consumes can help her make better food choices. It's easier than ever before to know how much trans-fat we consume; the United States FDA has required that all food companies must list the amount of trans-fat in their products since 2006.

Weight-Gain, Weight-Loss Truths

If all this business about reading labels is confusing, don't worry. Health professionals don't recommend that teens actually count out every Calorie they consume. The truth is that it takes a long time to gain weight, and it will take some time to lose it. Over time, overweight people have consumed more Calories than they expended or used. That's how they gained weight. In order to lose it, they'll have to use more Calories than they take in so their bodies will be forced to use accumulated fat cells for energy.

There are two ways to do this: get more exercise in order to expend the incoming Calories and reduce the amount of Calories consumed in the first place. By reading labels, we know that ice cream, for example, has a lot more Calories than, say, a bowl of steamed broccoli. Does this mean an overweight person always has to choose broccoli over ice cream? No, it doesn't. Overweight people can still indulge in ice cream once in a while as long as they offset the Calories by also consuming lots of fresh vegetables, fruits, and complex carbohydrates, which are lower in fat and Calories. (We will cover this more in chapter 4.)

Weight Gain, Weight Loss Myths

Many common myths surrounding weight loss exist. We will cover some of the myths about "crash" and "fad" diets in later chapters, but to understand how the body loses weight it's important to look at some myths about how the body does it:

Ice cream is high in Calories.

Weight Management

- Myth #1: If I skip breakfast, I will lose weight.
- Myth #2: If I don't eat at night, I will lose weight.
- Myth #3: If I work out in the morning instead of eating, my METABOLISM (that is, the amount of energy or Calories a body burns to maintain itself in its resting state) will increase throughout the day, making me burn more Calories.

First of all, there is no evidence that skipping meals actually helps people lose weight. In fact, health professionals have found that people who skip meals tend to overeat when they do finally get around to eating. Remember, it's not how much we eat, but what we eat and our levels of exercise that determines how our bodies will use the Calories. Also, if we skip breakfast, we may feel light-headed and have a hard time concentrating in class or during exercise. Teens need to eat breakfast in order to make it through the morning at top performance.

Myth #2 refers to the widespread belief that our bodies' metabolisms slow down at night, making it hard for us to burn Calories while we sleep—and therefore, it's better not to eat at all after a certain time, like 7:00 at night. This is not true; the fact is, our bodies work all the time, even while we are sleeping. Our hearts are beating, our blood is circulating, and our brains are working, all of which means we are still burning Calories. In other words, it doesn't really matter what time of day we consume Calories; what matters, again, is how many Calories we consume and how many we burn over a period of a week, or a month, or longer, not just in one day.

The problem of late-night snacking has more to do with the fact that many people sit and watch TV late at night and engage in "mindless snacking"—that is, eating potato chips, cookies, and other high-fat snacks while sitting around. This is not a good idea at any time of day, but it's a habit of many North Americans, and it's a habit that is worth breaking.

How Does the Body Lose Weight?

An early-morning bike ride—or other exercise—will help raise your metabolism so that you burn more Calories throughout the day.

Weight Management

As for myth #3, again, not eating breakfast, or even postponing it, will not increase a person's metabolism. Exercise is what increases metabolism, any time of day or night. So while it's true that the work-out first thing in the morning is what raises someone's metabolism, not eating won't make a difference, and in fact, may lower a person's blood sugar, making her feel more light-headed and therefore decreasing her productivity in the work-out. It's best to eat a healthy, well-balanced meal in the morning to avoid light-headedness and the possibility of over-eating later in the day. Work-outs in the morning are fine; just don't forgo eating a good breakfast first.

Ultimately, what helps someone lose weight is increasing physical activity to help burn Calories, and reducing the amount of Calories consumed. Reducing added weight from fat and increasing exercise also improves a person's health. Numerous health benefits can be had by losing as little as five to 10 percent of a person's body weight, with the goal being to achieve and maintain a healthy weight overall.

3

Why Do I Need to Lose Weight?

When you think of overweight people, what comes to mind? Do you think of the way overweight people look? Do you think about how they may feel? What about the health risks involved with being overweight? Sometimes our culture judges overweight people harshly, supposing that they are not as bright or educated or likeable as thinner people. This is a type of PREJUDICE; thinking like this is buying

Weight Management

into a STEREOTYPE that's just as false as any of the stereotypes about ethnic groups or gender.

Extremely intelligent people, funny people, likeable people, and talented people can be overweight. Being overweight says nothing about a person's INHERENT value. If you're overweight, you are just as good and have as much to offer as any thinner person. But being overweight is a health risk. In fact, it's one of our society's most serious medical problems.

Many people want to lose weight so they can change the way they look. If they lose their extra pounds, it's true that they may feel better about themselves, both mentally and physically. However, losing weight just to look a certain way shouldn't be the main reason for someone to change his diet and exercise more. There are very real health consequences of being overweight, and in this chapter we'll discuss them at length.

General Overview of Obesity's Health Risks

Overweight people are at an increased risk for developing health problems such as heart disease, stroke, diabetes, certain types of cancer, gout (joint pain caused by excess uric acid), and gallbladder disease. Being overweight can also cause problems such as osteoarthritis (wearing away of the joints) and sleep apnea (interrupted breathing while sleeping). The more overweight someone is, the likelier he is to develop one or more of these conditions.

There is hope, however. Studies show that losing as little as ten to twenty pounds can greatly improve a person's health. For many people, the challenge of losing a lot of weight is very daunting, so they instead focus on losing weight in small increments. These people are actually doing their bodies a great service by losing a little bit of weight at a time. Health experts recommend weight loss of no more than two pounds per week.

Heart Disease and Stroke

Heart disease is the leading cause of death and stroke is the third leading cause.

Coronary heart disease (or coronary artery disease) is a narrowing of the small blood vessels that supply blood and oxygen to the heart (coronary arteries). Coronary heart disease usually results from a buildup of fatty material and PLAQUE, otherwise known as atherosclerosis. This buildup is the result of diets high in fat and cholesterol (a soft, waxy substance produced in the liver and also present in foods from animal products). Too much fat and cholesterol in a person's diet can narrow the coronary arteries, and the flow of blood to the heart can slow or stop. The disease can cause chest pain, shortness of breath, heart attack, or other symptoms—including death. In general, coronary heart disease affects mostly adults. However, studies show that overweight and obese teens are at increased risk of developing coronary heart disease by their late teens.

A stroke is an interruption of the blood supply to any part of the brain, resulting in damaged brain tissue. Most strokes are due to blood clots that block blood flow. Bleeding into the brain occurs if a blood vessel ruptures or if there is a significant injury. Like heart disease, a leading cause of stroke is atherosclerosis.

Overweight people are more likely to have high blood pressure, which is a major risk factor for heart disease and stroke. Also, overweight and obese people tend to have higher levels of cholesterol and triglycerides (blood fats) in their blood, which can lead to atherosclerosis. In short, being overweight or obese makes it hard for a person's heart and blood vessels to do their jobs properly.

Reducing weight by as little as 10 percent can often decrease a person's chance of developing coronary heart disease or stroke by improving how her heart works. Losing weight helps to lower

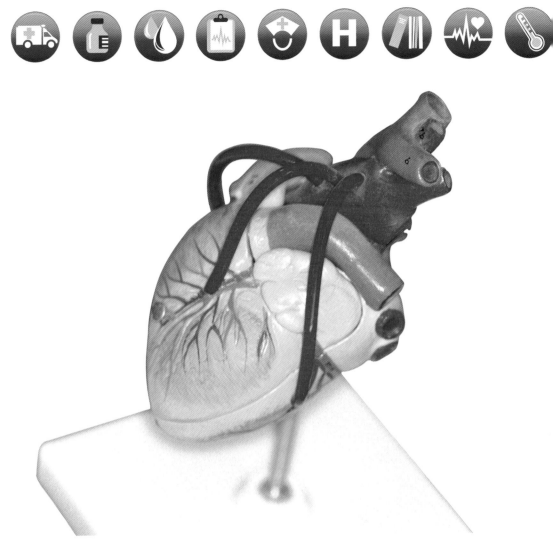

Obesity can damage the heart.

blood pressure and lowers the levels of blood cholesterol and tri-glycerides.

Diabetes

Type II diabetes, or noninsulin dependent diabetes mellitus, used to be known as "adult-onset" diabetes because it generally occurred in adults over the age of forty-five. Now however, due

A medical practitioner can help teens develop a healthy weight management program.

Weight Management

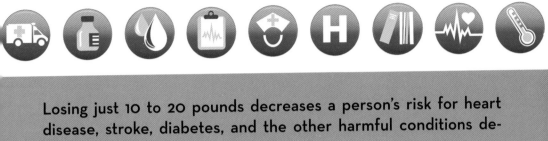

to the increase in overweight and obese children, type 2 diabetes is striking teens and even younger children in record numbers. Overweight people are twice as likely to develop Type II diabetes than people who are not overweight.

Diabetes is a life-long disease marked by high levels of sugar in the blood. Type II diabetes reduces the body's ability to control blood sugar. Basically, when a person digests food, a sugar called glucose enters the bloodstream. Glucose is fuel for the body. An organ in our bodies called the pancreas makes a hormone called insulin to help move the glucose through the bloodstream into muscle, fat, and liver cells where the body uses it as fuel.

Diabetes can be caused by too little insulin, resistance to insulin, or both. For people who already have diabetes, their bodies cannot control the level of blood sugar in their bodies, which in turn can cause all kinds of problems, including heart disease, kidney disease, stroke, blindness, and early death.

Losing weight and exercising more can help a person reduce his risk for developing this disease. For teens who already have Type II diabetes, losing weight and becoming more physically active can help their bodies control their blood-sugar levels. Doctors and other health care providers can help overweight diabetics develop a plan for weight management and exercise. Losing weight and exercise may even allow people with diabetes to take less medication.

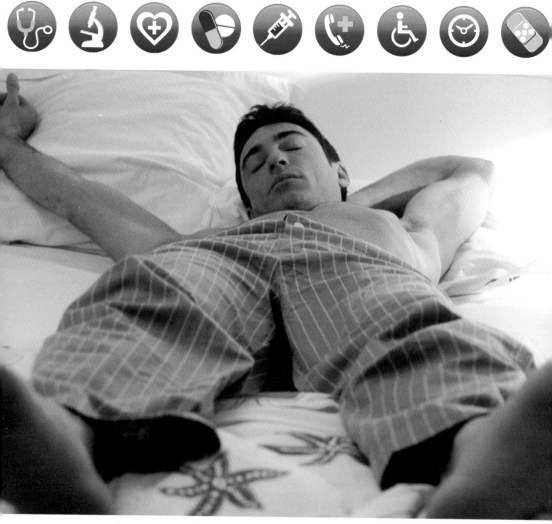

Losing weight can improve the quality of sleep.

Cancer

Several types of cancer are associated with being overweight or obese. For women, the risks include breast cancer, uterine cancer, cervical cancer, ovarian cancer, and cancer of the colon. Men who are overweight are at greater risk of developing colon cancer, as well as cancer of the rectum and prostate. People can reduce their risk for these types of cancers by getting regular exercise, eating a well-balanced diet that is low in fat and high in fiber, and having regular physical check-ups.

Cancer attacks healthy cells in the body and produces tumors that affect the way a person's organs can do their jobs. Hundreds of thousands of people die every year in the United States and Canada from cancer.

Sleep Apnea

Sleep apnea is a condition that causes people to stop breathing for short periods during sleep. It is a serious condition that is closely associated with being overweight. According to health experts, sleep apnea may cause daytime sleepiness and even heart failure. Weight loss, even small amounts, can improve sleep apnea.

Osteoarthritis

Overweight people are at increased risk of developing this common joint disorder, which affects the knees, hips, and lower back. The extra weight an overweight person carries puts a burden on these joints and wears away at the cartilage (the tissues that cushion the joints) that protects them.

Again, weight loss can decrease the stress placed on a person's joints and may improve the symptoms of osteoarthritis.

Gout

Gout is a joint disease caused by high levels of uric acid in the blood. Uric acid is a waste product that is found in blood and urine. Too much uric acid in a person's blood can sometimes form into solid stone or crystal masses that become lodged in the joints, causing painful arthritis. Overweight people are more at risk of developing gout, and the risk increases the more overweight a person is.

Overeating can provide short-term comfort—but in the long run, losing weight tends to improve self-esteem.

Weight Management

Gallbladder Disease

Overweight people also have an increased risk for gallbladder disease and gallstones. The gallbladder is a sac underneath the liver. It stores and concentrates bile (a thick digestive fluid), which is produced in the liver and aids in the digestion of fats. Bile is released from the gallbladder in response to food, especially fats, in the upper small intestine. People who are even moderately overweight or obese are at increased risk of having gallbladder problems. When you are overweight, the liver produces too much cholesterol, overloading the bile and increasing the risk for gallstones.

Losing Weight and Self-Esteem

In addition to reducing health risks, losing weight may help a person feel better about how she looks and feels. Many teens struggle with self-esteem (even those who are thin!), and overweight teens are often teased about their appearance. Overweight teens such as Jenny have found support and encouragement from their parents and friends. Jenny also found that working with her health care provider to set goals for herself that she could reach made her feel better about her progress. Losing weight takes time and commitment to a healthier lifestyle. As we will see in the next chapter, "fad" and "crash" diets don't work. What helps people lose weight is eating a variety of healthy foods in moderation and getting regular exercise.

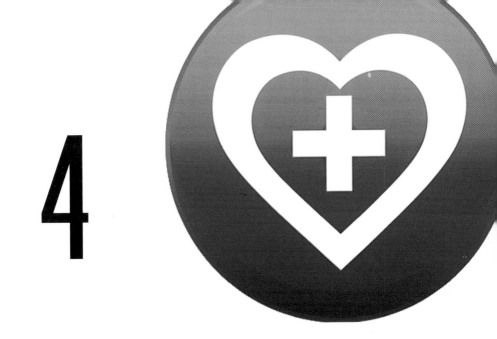

4

Why Don't Diets Work?

Many people in our society often look for a "quick fix" to their problems. We want easy solutions and we want to see them now. We don't like to wait for results. Perhaps that is why fad diets, such as the Atkins and other low-carbohydrate diets, or the "Cabbage Soup Diet" seem appealing to many North Americans.

Fad diets often promote rapid weight loss through eliminating one type of food or overemphasizing certain foods over others. Crash diets promote rapid weight loss and encourage eating less than our bodies need to make it through the day. But not only are diets such as these not effective in the long term, some of them can be unhealthy.

According to the FDA, fad diets "are fundamentally different from federal nutrition guidelines and are not recommended for losing weight." Why? Because they usually overemphasize eating one food or particular food group instead of eating a balanced diet. Fad diets can sometimes help people lose weight at first, but they rarely have a permanent effect, because the person eventually goes back to his regular eating patterns and gains back all the pounds he lost.

Low-Carb, High-Protein Diets

One of the most popular fad diets in today's society is some version of the high-protein, low-carbohydrate diet. The idea behind these diets is that restricting intake of carbohydrates will force the body to burn fats instead of carbohydrates for energy. Apparently, if there are no carbohydrates to burn, the body will burn fats instead, and the more fats you burn, the more you lose.

These diets may sound good in theory, except that lowering carbohydrate intake also makes the kidneys work harder to get rid of the excess waste products from the additional proteins and fats. These waste products are called ketones, and too many of them in the bloodstream (called ketosis) can cause the body to produce high levels of uric acid, which is a risk factor for developing gout and kidney stones (a condition in which crystalline stones are formed in the kidney, causing a lot of pain). Ketosis can be especially risky for diabetics because it can speed the progression of diabetic renal disease, a disease of the urinary tract.

Low-carb diets focus on meat, eggs, and other foods high in proteins.

According to health experts, low-carb diets' health considerations include the following:

- Low-carb diets are often higher in animal products, which have more saturated fats and cholesterol.
- Diets high in saturated fats may lead to increased risk for prostate or other cancers.
- High protein diets may jeopardize bone health, since excess consumption of animal proteins causes excretion of calcium in urine.
- A diet lacking in carbohydrates makes it difficult to exercise, especially in higher intensity or longer duration AEROBIC EXERCISES. These activities help to prevent and treat heart disease, high blood pressure, diabetes, arthritis, and some forms of cancer. They are also important factors in healthy weight management. Remember, weight loss is a combination of a balanced diet and exercise.
- High-protein diets may cause kidney damage.
- Gastrointestinal disorders (such as constipation and irritable bowel syndrome) may be worsened by a high fat, low-carb diet. High-protein diets often lack a variety of fruits, vegetables, and whole grains that contain a multitude of beneficial substances such as fiber and many vitamins and minerals. Fiber helps prevent constipation and other gastrointestinal disorders.

Not all experts agree on what is the best way to lose weight. Some research does indicate that low-carb diets may be effective. In general, however, most health experts agree that a well-balanced diet that includes a variety of low-fat, high-fiber foods, coupled with exercise and lots of physical activity, is the best

Don't go on a diet that promises that you will reach your weight-loss goals rapidly. You may lose weight quickly on these temporary diets, but it will be mostly water and hard to keep off once you return to your regular eating habits. Healthy weight management involves changing your eating habits and getting exercise on a regular basis and for life.

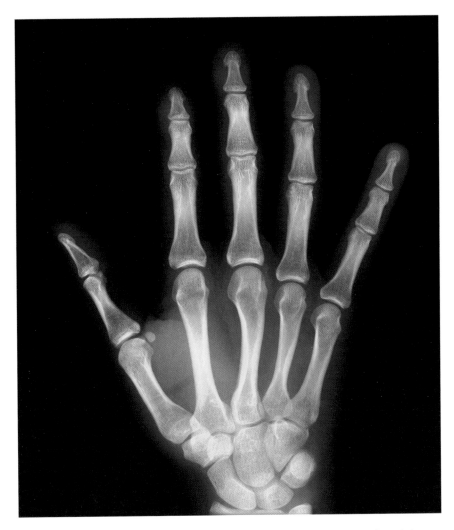

Long-term high-protein diets may damage bone health.

Why Don't Diets Work?

A healthy diet includes fruit, vegetables, grains, and proteins.

Weight Management

way to maintain a healthy body weight. Getting together with a doctor or other health care provider can provide a person with information on a diet and exercise plan that is right for him.

What Are Carbohydrates and Why Do I Need Them?

Carbohydrates have been getting a bad rap lately, but they are actually very good for us. They provide energy and fuel for our bodies and brains.

In short, carbohydrates are either "simple" or "complex." Simple carbohydrates are made up of one or two sugar molecules. The three single-sugar molecules are known as monosaccharides—glucose, fructose, and galactose—and they are found in fruits and vegetables, table sugars, and milk and milk products. These single sugars combine with each other to form disaccharides—two-molecule sugars—which are sucrose, lactose, and maltose. Complex carbohydrates, also known as starch and fiber, are polysaccharides (many sugars). Basically, they are long chains of sugar molecules, found in plant-based, unprocessed foods such as brown rice, sweet potatoes, beans, and grains.

Foods containing both simple and complex carbohydrates—such as fruits, vegetables, and whole grains—provide many nutrients, vitamins, and minerals we need in our diets. Complex carbohydrates also provide fiber, which the body needs to aid digestion. We do need to watch the amount of carbohydrates we take in from highly processed and sweetened foods such as white breads, cookies, ice cream, and cakes. Whole-grain foods are healthier alternatives.

A whole grain is a grain that has all parts of the original kernel intact, meaning it contains the fiber-rich bran, the nutrient rich germ, and the starchy endosperm. When a grain is refined,

the bran and germ are removed, and the flour is made from the endosperm. Most of the fiber, protein, and a number of vitamins and minerals are removed, too, and certain chemicals called phytochemicals are tossed out with the bran and germ. These plant chemical nutrients play important roles in our health. The endosperm does contain some nutrients, but not as much as the original kernel.

The bad news is that most commercially prepared breads and bread products such as cereals are made from refined grains rather than whole grains. The good news is that there are many products that contain whole grains.

Other Popular Weight Loss Plans: Do They Work?

Television and magazine advertisements often bombard us with slick ads for diet plans, diet pills, and weight-loss supplements. Many companies will make large profits if we buy their products or sign up for their classes. Weight-loss companies often claim we can lose weight without exercising or changing our lifestyle in any way.

Teenagers are often pressured to lose weight and to look a certain way. For someone who truly needs to lose weight, improving their eating habits and exercising regularly will help them more than any diet plan advertised on TV or in a glossy magazine.

In general, the diets advertised on TV fall into two categories: diets that drastically reduce a person's intake of Calories or eliminate an entire food group, and diets that require a person to take dietary supplements. Some diets advocate for virtual starvation—crash diets—and any diet that requires eating fewer Calories than a person needs to get through the day can be dangerous to his health. A diet that is too low in Calories can cause feelings of sleepiness and LETHARGY, and will not provide

Weight Management

Why Don't Diets Work?

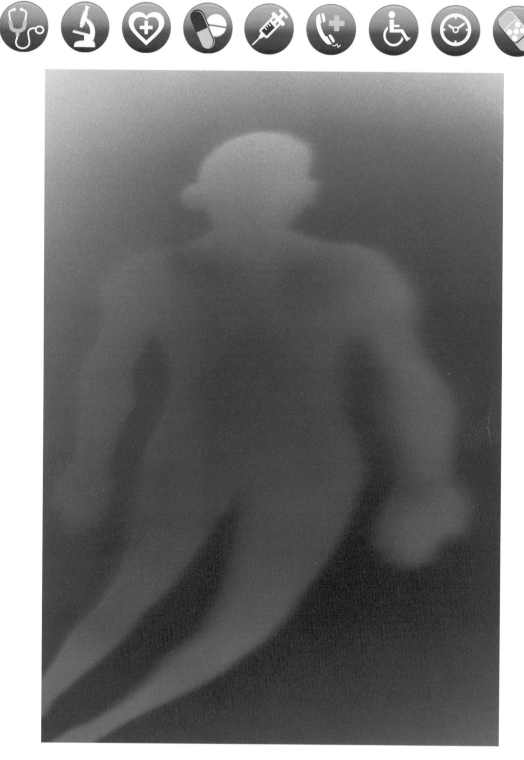

The diet industry appeals to Americans' obsession with body image.

Weight Management

enough energy a busy student needs to make it through class, let alone to get the necessary physical activity for good health.

Frankly, going on a low-Calorie diet may make a person drop a few pounds quickly, but it's actually mostly water he is losing, not fat. According to Dr. Steven Dowshen, the Chief Medical Editor at KidsHealth.org, when someone starves herself of Calories or fat by going on a rapid weight-loss dieting plan, her body's response is to dump water. Dr. Dowshen says, "Unfortunately, what these weight loss plans don't tell you is that your body will just suck this lost water back up like a sponge once you start eating more Calories again."

Other diets that advocate eliminating almost an entire food group, such as the low-carb diets we discussed previously, cannot provide people with all the vitamins and minerals we need.

THE YO-YO DIETING SYNDROME

Many people diet, and diet, and diet. They decide to lose weight, go on a diet, and reach their weight-loss goals. Then, they gain the weight back. So, they go on a diet, lose the weight, gain it back. Are you sensing a pattern here? This is called yo-yo dieting, and some doctors feel that years of this behavior may be more dangerous than being slightly overweight.

Most people who yo-yo diet will find that they gain more weight back each time. Why? It's your body's defense mechanism against starvation. When you deprive your body of the amount of food that it is used to, your metabolism slows down. The body is saving the stored up fat in case you never feed it again. So, you find yourself weighing more than you did before dieting.

Similarly, a diet that advocates no fat is not healthy. A teenager's body still needs a certain amount of fat; in fact, from 25 to 35 percent of his total daily caloric intake should come from fat.

Rarely will a diet that forces a drastic change in eating habits for only a short while have a life-long, positive impact on anyone's health. For one thing, what will happen when the diet is over? Eventually, the person on the diet will go back to her old eating habits and gain back all the weight she's lost. Our bodies are simply not designed to lose pounds quickly.

In order to keep weight off, a change in lifestyle is in order. The overweight teen will need to eat differently, not just for a short period of time, but for life. The good news is that maintaining a healthy weight involves no starvation and no pills that could make someone sick. It simply involves eating a healthy diet that includes lots of delicious foods and getting exercise, which can also be fun if done with friends or family.

Dietary Supplements

We've all seen the ads that claim we can lose weight if we simply buy the product being advertised and then swallow the pills. The ads usually claim that a doctor has discovered some new secret formula that melts pounds away without any real effort on our part. If you're someone who has a hard time believing the ads, you're right to be skeptical. There's little evidence that dietary supplements or pills have the miracle effects they claim—and in fact, there's evidence that many supplements can be dangerous.

Dietary supplements can include vitamins, minerals, amino acids, herbs, and plants, or any concentration, extract, or combination of these. They can be purchased in gel capsules, liquid, powder, or pill forms. The safety of these products is always questionable because the FDA does not check on the safety of

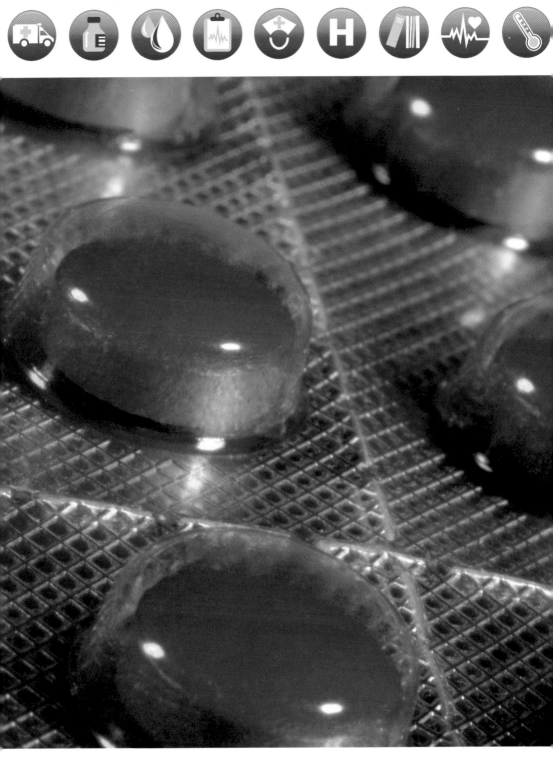

Dietary supplements claim to offer "miracle cures" for obesity.

Why Don't Diets Work?

dietary supplements before they are sold. The FDA has to wait for reports of problems before it can investigate and ban a dietary supplement.

Despite the evidence that dietary supplements are not effective and may not be safe, many myths persist about their EF-FICACY. These myths include:

Myth: Supplements can make me a better athlete.

Fact: Many athletes take dietary supplements to improve their performance, but these claims are often exaggerated and not based on scientific evidence. Some of them, such as anabolic steroids (man-made hormones similar to testosterone), are unsafe and illegal. Other athletic supplements, such as powdered amino acids, are expensive and don't provide anything that can't be found in a well-balanced diet.

Myth: Natural supplements can't hurt because they're natural.

Fact: Not only can "all-natural" supplements be dangerous, they can even be deadly. For example, the herb ephedra speeds up the metabolism, helping people to lose weight faster. Unfortunately, it can also cause dizziness, jitters, insomnia, and heart problems. Some people have even suffered strokes, heart attacks, and SEIZURES.

Myth: I need to take additional vitamins and supplements.

Fact: Eating a well-balanced diet provides all the necessary vitamins and minerals. However, it's fine to take a regular one-a-day multivitamin, as long as it's taken in addition to eating a well-balanced diet.

IT'S A MATTER OF CHOICE

Sometimes when you're watching your weight it might seem as though you can't have anything that you like. Of course you can, sometimes. It's a question of moderation and making choices.

It's pizza night, and you long for the taste of that crunchy crust, the pizza sauce, and yes, cheese. Try making your own pizza using reduced fat mozzarella cheese. Order a veggie pizza instead of the higher fat pepperoni, sausage, or ground beef versions. Add pineapple and some hot peppers for that special pizzazz.

Ahh, you'll have salad with lots of healthy greens and other vegetables. But, your favorite salad dressing is the creamy kind. Try making your own using yogurt and fresh herbs and spices.

It's hot and you want ice cream, but you've already splurged and would like something healthier. Try a smoothie. Blend together frozen or fresh fruit with frozen yogurt. Or, blend frozen fruit with ice and a little milk. Pour into a tall glass, add a straw (and a little umbrella) and live it up! It's cold, refreshing, and healthier than ice cream.

Your new weight management goals give you the chance to learn new skills. Experiment with food and recipes. Perhaps it will lead to a new career choice!

Walking regularly is part of a healthy lifestyle.

Weight Management

Diet Plan Diagnosis: Creating a Healthy, Safe Diet

As we've already discussed in this chapter, those weight-loss plans we see advertised on TV and in teen magazines don't work. So what does work?

Health experts in general agree that in order to lose extra weight and then to maintain a healthy weight, a well-balanced diet coupled with exercise does the trick. Unfortunately, there are no short-term answers or magic pills for being overweight or obese. A change in eating habits and lifestyle to include regular physical activity is what's going to work. Turning physical activity into a regular habit helps teens to maintain a healthy weight for the rest of their lives.

The next two chapters discuss how to decrease Calories by eating a healthy diet and how to increase burning those Calories through exercise. Of course, it's always best to visit a health care provider for a personalized diet and exercise plan.

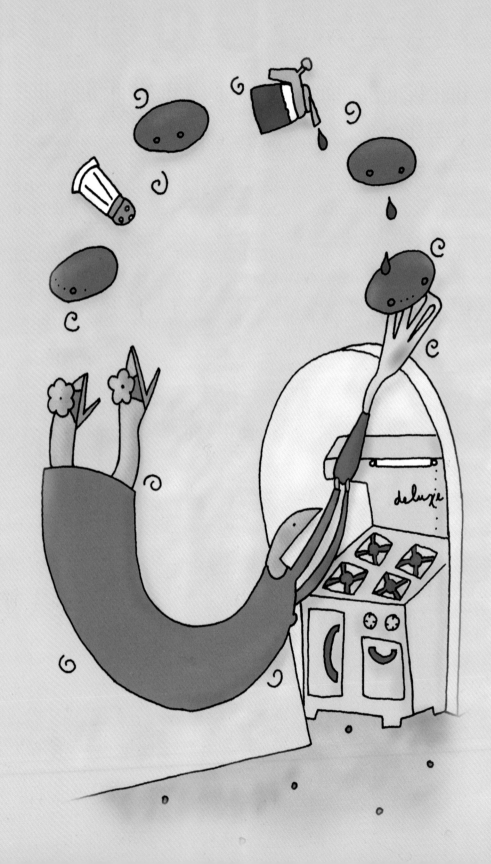

5

How Can I Decrease
My Caloric Intake?

t seems like common sense that the way we'd decrease our Calories is to eat less. To some extent that's true, but if you've read this far, you also know by now that eating fewer Calories than you need is not healthy. The FDA recommends a daily intake of between 2,000 and 2,500 Calories. The exact number will depend on people's level of physical activity and whether they are male or female. Also, very obese people may need to consume fewer Calories overall until they reach their ideal weight. So, we don't necessarily need to eat less to lose weight; we just need to eat less of the foods that are high in Calories.

You may find it helpful to think about what a typical daily or weekly diet is like for you. For many North Americans, our diets regularly include fast food, potato chips, French fries, cheeseburgers, ice cream, chocolate bars, candy, sweet cereals, white bread and crackers, and lots of dairy and meat products. None of these foods are totally bad for us—the trick is to consume them in moderation and, more importantly, to replace them with healthier foods.

Fortunately, many stores now stock healthier versions of some of the most popular snack foods on the market. Since teens are most likely not the family's grocery shopper or food purchaser, they may have to get their parents in on their new eating habits. This, of course, may prove very difficult, especially if your parents are also in the habit of eating high-fat foods. Perhaps they could read this book with you and meet with your health care provider or school counselor for ideas.

Many health experts recommend that parents join their children in eating healthier foods and getting exercise together. But even if parents are only willing to purchase healthier foods, that's a good start. Just remember that losing weight and maintaining a healthy weight takes a long time, and it can be difficult to change when everyone around us doesn't. There are unhealthy food choices everywhere to tempt us. Many teens find support for changing their diets through friends or even support groups. You may want to ask your health care provider or guidance counselor at school for references.

How and When Should I Eat?

As previously discussed, fad or crash dieting is not recommended. But many people still have questions about how much and how often they can eat. Should we eat three meals a day, or five or six small meals? Should we not eat at bedtime? Should we avoid snacking throughout the day?

Many North Americans eat fast food frequently.

How Can I Decrease My Caloric Intake?

Popcorn without butter and salt can be a healthy snack alternative.

Weight Management

In general, there is no "right" or "wrong" time to eat. Nor is there any magic time when not eating will help a person lose weight. Most health experts recommend eating when we are hungry and avoiding overeating. The number of meals people have per day and when they eat will depend on their schedules and the number of Calories they want to take in, as recommended by their health care professionals.

Skipping meals is not a good idea! People who skip meals or snacks are more likely to get overly hungry—or "starving!" as they might say—and that can lead to overeating.

As will be reinforced throughout this book (if you haven't noticed already), it's what we eat and how much physical activity we get that will help us lose weight and maintain a healthy weight. So read on for more information about the best foods to avoid—or indulge in only moderately—and the best foods to make up the mainstay of a diet.

What to Eat Less Of

The foods on this list are common staples in the North American diet. In order to lose weight, it's not necessary to avoid them completely, but for people accustomed to eating these foods regularly, a shift in how much and what types of foods they eat will help melt the pounds off.

- FAST FOODS: Fast-food outlets are notorious for serving high-fat, high-sodium, and high-cholesterol foods. For example, just one Whopper® with cheese from Burger King has around 800 Calories in it and a whopping 48 grams of fat (18 grams from saturated fat). Just to put that in perspective, if you want to eat about 2,000 Calories a day, and you ate a Whopper with large fries (500 Calories) and a me-

dium coke (200 Calories) for lunch, that wouldn't leave you many choices for dinner (let alone breakfast or snacks). That would mean that you'd have to stick to a breakfast, dinner, and snacks that all combined, would total about 510 Calories. You can, however, eat healthier at fast-food restaurants. You can choose salads and sandwiches that aren't fried and contain much less fat. Remember, though, that creamy salad dressing, cheese, fried croutons, and that "secret sauce" can turn low-fat alternatives into the type of high-fat foods you're trying to avoid.

- WHOLE-DAIRY PRODUCTS: The bad news is that these dairy products are very high in fat and cholesterol. The good news is that there are plenty of alternatives. Dairy is definitely one of the products in the grocery store with a variety of low-fat versions of the same tasty higher-fat products. Eliminating dairy altogether is not a good idea as it's a good source of calcium and vitamin D. Some things worth trying instead of whole dairy products are low-fat sour cream, lite cream cheese (this one is still high in fat, but if you eat a lot of cream cheese, the lite version does help), skim or 1-percent milk, low-fat cheeses, and substituting frozen yogurt or frozen dairy-free treats such as Italian ice or fruit popsicles for ice cream.

- CURED MEATS: These include ham, bacon and salt pork, sausages, and lunch meats such as salami, corned beef, and bologna. They are extremely high in fat, cholesterol, and sodium. Some vegetarian versions of these foods taste different, but good in their own way. It's worth trying some different brands to see if there may be anything palatable to you, as they are much lower in fat and contain no cholesterol. Only animal products naturally contain cholesterol.

Weight Management

Cured and processed meats are high in fat and sodium.

- PROCESSED MEATS: Bologna, ham, hotdogs, and other lunch meat products made from pork or beef tend to be very high in fat, cholesterol, and sodium. Try chicken or turkey breast meat instead. Some vegetarian hotdogs on the market are actually pretty tasty. They are low in fat and sodium and have no cholesterol.
- SALTY SNACKS: Snacks such as potato chips, corn chips, popcorn with lots of salt and butter, cheese or peanut butter crackers, and processed cheeses all contain high amounts of saturated fats, trans-fat, and sodium. Snacks can make up a large chunk of your daily Calories, so it's best to snack on low-fat foods that offer a high nutritional value.

- SWEET SNACKS: Candy bars, ice cream cones, packaged cookies and brownies, shakes, malts, pies, and other "treats" such as these often contain high amounts of fat and offer little nutritional value. Read on for some alternatives to these foods.

What to Eat More Of

According to the American Heart Association, a healthy diet consists of several servings of grains per day (and they recommend at least half of those servings come from whole grains), four or five servings of fruits and vegetables, two or three servings of dairy products, and six ounces of meat or other protein products.

When you're counting Calories, you can generally eat as many vegetables as you wish, as most of them are low in fat (or contain no fat at all). Vegetables, then, make a great healthy snack.

- WHOLE GRAINS: As discussed in the last chapter, these include oats (oatmeal), popcorn, brown rice, and whole grain breads, cereals and crackers (check the label). Grains that aren't whole include white rice, white flour, most breads and bread products, and many cereals. See chapter 4 for some common products made from whole grains.
- FRESH FRUITS: For a change, throw an apple in your book bag instead of a candy bar for that quick after school snack. Try strawberries on your cereal, bananas in your oatmeal, or just plain oranges and clementines, pineapple, and grapefruit. In the summer, enjoy fresh peaches, apricots, blueberries, cherries, and other berries. Dried fruits can make a good snack, but be careful, many of them are high in sugar.

Weight Management

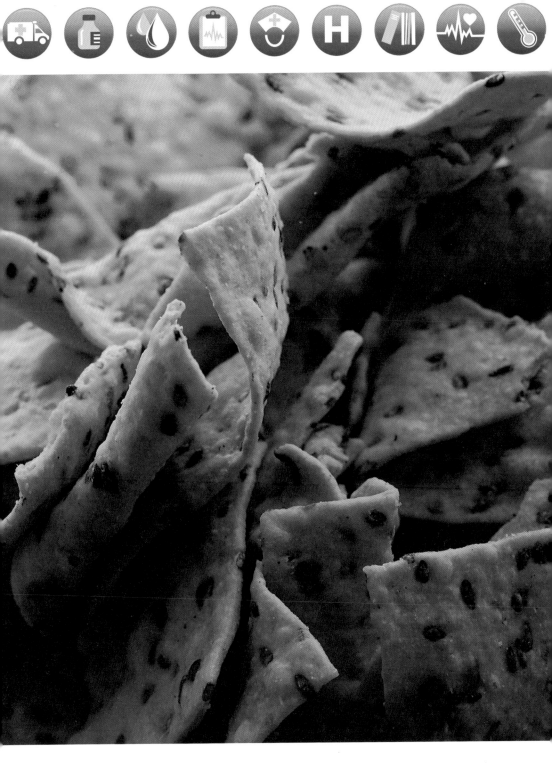

Whole-grain, baked chips are healthy alternatives to salty, fried snacks.

How Can I Decrease My Caloric Intake?

Low-fat yogurt is a healthy snack option.

Weight Management

- FRESH VEGETABLES: Fresh salads made with lots of green leafy vegetables—especially dark green leafy ones—are wonderful as a side dish or a full meal and are very nutritious, just avoid the creamy dressings and look for something made with oil, vinegar, and herbs and spices. Other vegetable ideas include carrot or celery sticks, cucumber slices, and fresh snap peas. Try steamed vegetables with dinner instead of canned or frozen ones. Other ways of incorporating more vegetables into your diet include ordering veggie pizzas instead of meat, tossing vegetables into soups or stews, adding veggies to spaghetti sauce, shredding carrots or mushrooms on your salad, and making omelets with vegetables in them.
- LOW-FAT DAIRY: Start by asking your parents to purchase low-fat versions of the dairy you eat most, such as sour cream, cream cheese, cottage cheese, and milk. Eventually, you may be able to switch entirely to low-fat versions or give some of these dairy products up entirely. Try low-fat yogurt either as a snack or as a meal with fresh fruit and low-Calorie bread for toast. Plain, nonfat yogurt can also be used as a substitute for sour cream or milk in some recipes, and yogurt has many beneficial cultures. Switch to one-percent or skim milk. Exchange ice cream for nonfat popsicles or fruit smoothies.
- LOW-FAT MEATS: Instead of having a beef and pork hot dog, try a turkey dog, a chicken dog, or a vegetarian hot dog. Chicken breasts are low in fat and sodium and make great sandwiches and meals. Turkey is low in fat but high in sodium.
- SNACKS: Snacks can comprise a large portion of your daily nutrients and fat, so choose snacks that are low in fat, sugar, and salt. Learn how to read labels so you know what you are eating. Some healthy snacks include:

Cooking a healthy meal together can be a fun way to spend time with your family and maintain a healthy lifestyle.

Weight Management

whole grain crackers with cheese, yogurt, fresh fruits or vegetables, smoothies, and whole grain cereals.

Eating a well-balanced diet means eating a diet that includes healthy, delicious foods. Instead of thinking of eating well as just another diet to suffer through, try thinking of its many benefits. For one, it can be a lot of fun to cook and try new recipes. For another, people who maintain a healthy weight feel better, and this can last for a person's whole life. Ultimately, feeling good about food and eating, getting exercise, and having fun will seem like second nature. There is really nothing sufferable about it.

6

How Can I Increase
My Caloric Output?

When Jenny changed her eating habits, she also changed her daily routine to include more exercise. Her doctor recommended that she begin exercising a little bit at first to avoid strain and to get used to a routine. Eventually, she was able to get to the point where she could exercise about five times per week for 30 minutes each time.

Swimming is a good aerobic exercise that burns calories.

Weight Management

Jenny's exercise program includes walking, swimming, and bicycling. She loves to swim, and eventually she joined a gym so she could use the pool; however, it isn't necessary for everyone who wants to exercise to join a gym. Jenny simply walked a lot at first, taking thirty-minute brisk walks, and then she started riding her bike to school instead of taking the bus. Now she rides her bike three times a week for at least a half hour, and swims at the gym at least once. She walks a lot more than she used to and has given up some TV time in order to do it.

Aerobic Exercise Burns Calories

"Aerobic" means "with oxygen" and any aerobic exercise includes a long duration of low to moderate difficulty using the large muscle groups of the body such as the legs, back, and arms. For people who want to or need to lose a lot of weight, the key is to do longer, more frequent aerobic sessions at an easier pace. Even though a more vigorous workout burns more Calories per minute than an easy effort, an extra 15 or 30 minutes of easy exercise will more than make up the difference, and it doesn't tire people out as much. Also, longer bouts of exercise burn proportionally more fat. Harder but shorter exercise draws more on carbohydrates, but for people who want to shed pounds, it's more important to burn fat Calories than carbohydrate Calories.

In addition to burning Calories and reducing body fat, aerobic exercise offers many other advantages, including reduced cholesterol and blood pressure, improved muscular endurance, and increased metabolism. Aerobic activities strengthen the heart and lungs, making them more durable and able to work more efficiently, which helps to improve the quality and quantity of life. It also gives people more energy to live life to the fullest.

Aerobic exercise also strengthens bones, ligaments, and tendons, and can reduce the risk of heart disease, vascular disease,

and diabetes. It's also good for people trying to quit smoking and can help prevent the weight gain that many people who quit smoking experience. Research shows that aerobic exercise reduces stress and can help combat depression.

Getting Started

It's always a good idea to check with a doctor or other health care provider before starting an exercise program. In general, some good goals to set are to:

- be able to exercise continuously for 45 to 60 minutes without strain, but while still increasing the heart rate. To do this, many people find that making their effort as easy as possible enables them to exercise for up to an hour.
- exercise aerobically five to seven times per week.
- try to do one or more long workouts per week.
- to reduce the amount of fats consumed each day. Remember, a gram of dietary fat contains nine Calories, whereas a gram of carbohydrates or proteins each contain only four Calories.

Setting goals helps people to stay on track for the long haul. Health experts don't recommend losing more than two pounds per week, so it may take a while before a very overweight or obese person sees a major difference. Try to remember that every little step helps, and that losing just 10 to 20 pounds makes a huge difference in an overweight person's health.

A Ten-Week Startup Program for Beginners

This is a good program for people new to exercising and recommended by physicians at Harvard Medical School. It begins with

Smoking increases the risk of heart and vascular diseases.

How Can I Increase My Caloric Output?

short workouts that gradually get longer. By week ten, the participants in the program swim, cycle, walk, or engage in some other form of aerobic activity for at least forty-five minutes four days a week. The fifth day on the schedule is an optional workout.

Every session should begin and end with five minutes of slow and easy walking (whether on a treadmill or on the sidewalk). These easy walks will prevent blood from "pooling" in the legs after exercise.

The guide to how hard the workout should be is called the "Rating of Perceived Exertion" (or RPE) method of gauging intensity:

Easy = 5 or less on the RPE scale
Steady = 5 to 7 on the RPE scale
Brisk = 7 or more on the RPE scale

Each person picks a number from 1 to 10 that corresponds to how hard they feel they are working. Number 1 is the easiest; it is something that someone could do for extended periods of time, such as watching television. Number 10 represents an all-out workout, such as running a marathon.

In order to get the best workout, the session (including warm-up and cool-down periods) should fall within the 5–8 range. Each person rates their own effort, numbering their workout sessions according to how they feel, how hard they're breathing, how fast their heart is beating, and so on. The numbers may change after a while. For example, someone jogs one mile around the track at school and rates that at an 8. After a few months, that workout may become a number 4, and the person could jog another half-mile or more to bring it up to an 8.

Weight Management

Here are the workout session recommendations:

WEEK 1:

Day 1	20 minutes	easy
Day 2	20 minutes	easy
Day 3	20 minutes	easy
Day 4	20 minutes	easy
Day 5	20 minutes	easy

WEEK 2:

Day 1	20 minutes	easy
Day 2	25 minutes	easy
Day 3	20 minutes	easy
Day 4	25 minutes	easy
Day 5	20 minutes	easy

WEEK 3:

Day 1	25 minutes	easy
Day 2	25 minutes	steady
Day 3	25 minutes	easy
Day 4	25 minutes	steady
Day 5	25 minutes	easy

WEEK 4:

Day 1	25 minutes	easy
Day 2	30 minutes	steady
Day 3	25 minutes	easy
Day 4	30 minutes	steady
Day 5	20 minutes	easy

WEEK 5:

Day 1	30 minutes	easy
Day 2	30 minutes	steady
Day 3	30 minutes	easy
Day 4	30 minutes	steady
Day 5	30 minutes	easy

WEEK 6:

Day 1	30 minutes	steady
Day 2	35 minutes	easy
Day 3	30 minutes	steady
Day 4	35 minutes	steady
Day 5	30 minutes	easy

WEEK 7:

Day 1	35 minutes	steady
Day 2	35 minutes	easy
Day 3	35 minutes	steady
Day 4	35 minutes	steady
Day 5	35 minutes	easy

WEEK 8:

Day 1	35 minutes	steady
Day 2	40 minutes	easy
Day 3	35 minutes	steady
	(optional: 10 minutes brisk)	
Day 4	40 minutes	steady
Day 5	35 minutes	easy

WEEK 9:

Day 1	40 minutes	steady
	(optional: 10 minutes brisk)	
Day 2	45 minutes	steady
Day 3	40 minutes	steady
	(optional: 10 minutes brisk)	
Day 4	45 minutes	steady
Day 5	40 minutes	easy

WEEK 10:

Day 1	45 minutes	steady
	(optional: 10 minutes brisk)	
Day 2	45 minutes	steady
Day 3	45 minutes	steady
	(optional: 10 minutes brisk)	
Day 4	45 minutes	steady
Day 5	45 minutes	easy

Fitting Exercise and Healthy Eating into a Busy Schedule

Most teens, like most everybody in North America, have busy lives. Between school, part-time jobs, after-school clubs or groups, sports, lessons, and being with our families and loved ones, people seem to have less time than ever before.

There are some simple ways of incorporating exercise into a daily routine, such as walking or riding a bike to school instead of taking the bus, and taking the stairs at every chance instead of an escalator or elevator. However, in order to exercise aero-

bically for at least twenty to forty-five minutes at a stretch, a little more commitment than just walking to school may be in order. Researchers have found that you don't have to do your exercise all at once, however, another option would be to exercise 10 minutes at a time, three times a day.

For people who watch a lot of TV or play a lot of video games, getting exercise is a worthwhile alternative. When we think about it, isn't it amazing how quickly an hour or more can pass while we sit in front of the television or computer? Most North Americans watch an average of four hours of television per day, probably because time can slip by so quickly while we channel surf. So, giving up a half hour or hour of TV time per day is one way of finding more time to exercise. We have to decide how important it is to take care of our bodies over how important a TV show is.

Some people like to get up early in the morning and make some time after breakfast for a quick jog or swim at the gym. Others find a sports team to join, either at school or through a county or city recreation program. People who can't afford to join a gym or don't want to join a sports team, can still get an aerobic workout just by walking briskly for at least 30 minutes per day, and perhaps increasing that to an hour or turning their walks into jogs.

For people who don't feel they would enjoy a traditional work-out session at the gym, two women in Boston started a workout called "Punk Rock Aerobics." The idea behind it is that the two women—Maura Jasper and Hilken Mancini—wanted to workout in an aerobics class but didn't like the music or the style of the clothes people wore. So, they became certified aerobics instructors and started teaching classes to punk rock music. They published a book so that others around the nation could start their own classes, and the idea can work for any

group of friends who wish to workout together to their own type of music.

Compulsive Exercise

Just one word of caution regarding exercise: there is such a thing as "too much." Many teens start out with good intentions for exercise, but can become obsessed with results and keep working out more and more to the point where they have an unhealthy COMPULSION with it.

Our bodies need exercise, but they also need rest. Over-exercising can lead to many injuries such as fractures and muscle strains. When a teen starts to put exercise above classes, friends, and other responsibilities, they may be developing a dependence on it.

Part of what can cause compulsive exercise is a distorted body image and low self-esteem. As we'll see in the next chapter, these attributes can lead to eating disorders. It's important to keep a positive self-image throughout the weight-loss process.

7

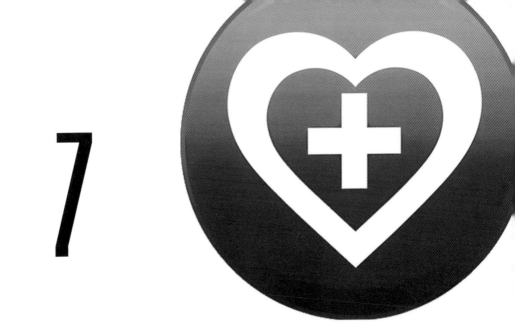

How Can I Avoid an Eating Disorder?

Sometimes, people who are within a healthy weight range still feel that they are "too fat" and put themselves at risk for developing an eating disorder by either starving themselves or overeating and then vomiting. Other people overeat regularly to avoid dealing with stress or complicated emotional problems, and they put themselves at risk for gaining too much weight too fast.

A person with an eating disorder often believes she is overweight even when she is not.

Weight Management

All three scenarios indicate a possible eating disorder. The primary eating disorders that affect millions of young Americans each year are: bulimia nervosa, which is characterized by eating large amounts of food and then throwing it up or using laxatives to avoid gaining weight; anorexia nervosa, characterized by an obsession with thinness that leads people to near starvation and compulsive exercise; and binge eating, which is extreme overeating without the vomiting or exercise.

All three eating disorders can cause serious health consequences. Fortunately, all three can be treated. Teens who think they may have an eating disorder or know someone who does can look for help from a parent, teacher, doctor, counselor, or friend.

What Are the Eating Disorders?

Anorexia Nervosa

Anorexia nervosa is characterized by a refusal to maintain a healthy body weight, intense fear of weight gain, and distorted body image. Inadequate Calorie intake or excessive and compulsive exercise can lead to severe weight loss. Current estimates show that approximately one to two percent of the female population suffers from anorexia, while 0.1 to 0.2 percent of males do.

Warning signs and symptoms of anorexia include:

- weight loss of 15 percent or greater below the expected weight
- self-starvation and intense fear of gaining weight
- self-perception of being fat, even when thin
- bizarre food behaviors, such as skipping meals, chew-

ing food and then spitting it out, and reading food labels compulsively
· inappropriate use of laxatives, enemas, or diuretics (water pills) in an effort to lose weight
· self-imposed food intake restrictions, often hidden
· denial of hunger
· extreme sensitivity to cold temperatures
· absence of menstruation
· skeletal muscle ATROPHY
· loss of fatty tissue
· loss of hair
· low blood pressure
· dental cavities and tooth decay from possible self-imposed vomiting
· blotchy or yellow skin
· depression or low self-esteem may be present
· dissatisfaction with body image and size even as weight loss continues
· denial that there is a problem

If the eating disorder continues, many complications may arise that can require hospitalization. The presence of any of the following suggests a severe eating disorder, and a doctor should be informed immediately:

· severe DEHYDRATION, which can lead to cardiovascular shock
· ELECTROLYTE imbalance
· cardiac ARRHYTHMIA related to the loss of cardiac muscle and electrolyte imbalance
· severe malnutrition

- thyroid gland deficiencies, which can lead to cold intolerance and constipation
- appearance of fine, baby-like hair covering the body (lanugo)
- bloating or EDEMA
- decrease in white blood cells, which can lead to increased susceptibility to infection
- OSTEOPOROSIS
- tooth erosion and decay
- seizures related to fluid imbalances due to excessive diarrhea or vomiting

Anorexia nervosa is pretty common, and you may know someone who suffers from it. If you do, it's best not to try to force the person to eat, but to approach her in a nonjudgmental way and let her know you are there to help her. You may wish to seek counseling from a parent or other trusted adult to help your friend. Your friend can't get over this disorder by herself; she must have the help of trained professionals. Only they can help her relearn how to eat properly, and, just as important, learn why she began this behavior pattern. Anorexia nervosa is a serious problem. In some cases, it can lead to death.

Bulimia Nervosa

Bulimia is as common than anorexia, affecting about 2 percent of young women. People with bulimia often cycle through periods of dieting, binge eating, and purging (vomiting after consuming large amounts of food). Symptoms of bulimia number far less than those for anorexia and include overeating or binge eating, self-induced vomiting, inappropriate use of diuretics or laxatives, and overachieving behavior. Young women who are

bulimic may consume up to 20,000 Calories in a very short period of time due to a feeling of being out of control. After the binge, they may feel guilty or ashamed, and then throw up the food to avoid gaining weight.

Complications of bulimia include:

- cavities, dental enamel erosion, and gum problems due to frequent vomiting
- low potassium levels leading to weakness (indicating that vomiting is occurring on a daily basis)
- tears or rupture of the ESOPHAGUS from repeated forced vomiting
- dehydration
- constipation, which may lead to a dependence on laxatives for normal bowel functioning
- HEMORRHOIDS
- heart rhythm abnormalities
- electrolyte imbalances from vomiting and laxative abuse

Again, if you know or think you know someone with bulimia, you can take steps to help your friend by offering a nonjudgmental ear. Criticizing someone with an eating disorder does more harm than good. Often, people with eating disorders deny they have a problem. They need to know that they can safely acknowledge their problem without being CHASTISED for it.

Binge Eating

Binge eating is characterized by overeating compulsively. Teens with a binge eating disorder consume large amounts of food and don't stop when they become full. They binge not just from time to time, as in overeating on a holiday, but they overeat regularly and feel powerless to stop. Teens who binge eat may con-

sume an entire bag of cookies and an entire bag of potato chips just while doing homework.

Teens who overeat regularly may do so because of stress, or feeling upset, hurt, or angry. They may find it comforting to eat the food, but afterward may feel guilty or ashamed about being out of control. Many teens who binge regularly do it because they are dealing with—or avoiding dealing with—difficult emotions.

The most common complication associated with binge eating is excessive weight gain, though not everyone who is overweight engages in binge eating. Bulimics may maintain their weight through vomiting or excessive use of laxatives even though they binge eat regularly. Binge eaters may also be more prone to unsafe dieting practices, falling prey to the claims in unhealthy diet ads and cycling through an unhealthy pattern of dieting, gaining weight, and dieting again.

For teens who are overweight because of a binge eating disorder, help is available through a combination of therapy and seeing a doctor regularly.

Causes of Eating Disorders

The exact causes of eating disorders can vary from person to person. Genetics, cultural influences, family dynamics, emotional disorders, and brain chemical abnormalities can all play a role.

Results from two studies show that anorexia is more common in people who have relatives with the disorder, suggesting that genetics are a link.

However, cultural influences and family dynamics cannot be overlooked. Consumer marketing and advertising place an emphasis on attractiveness associated with being thin. The models we see in teen magazines and on TV are often thinner than is really healthy. Athletes—in particular gymnasts, ballerinas,

A person with an eating disorder may see food as a dangerous lure she should resist.

Weight Management

and figure skaters—often are pressured to lose weight. With all this pressure around us to look a certain way, sometimes we just can't help but be influenced by the images and marketing campaigns that surround us.

Some teens with eating disorders such as binge eating have a history of using food as comfort, a coping mechanism that may be learned from their parents. Other disorders like anorexia can develop when parents put too much pressure on a child to be "perfect." Studies show that people afflicted with eating disorders tend to come from families with very high expectations of achievement and success. Sometimes parents can seem overly critical about a daughter's weight or appearance, encouraging her to engage in unhealthy eating habits that can lead to eating disorders.

Eating disorders can also develop because a teen feels a lack of control over things that are going on around her. She might not be able to control her popularity, fighting between her parents, or the illness or death of a beloved grandparent, but she can control how much she weighs. Unfortunately, in many cases this is done in an unhealthy manner that results in an eating disorder.

Several personality disorders, such as narcissim and avoidant personalities, have been linked with eating disorders. These personality disorders can play a role in the development and perpetuation of eating disorders, because people with these personality traits tend to be perfectionists and emotionally inhibited. Other links have been made between people with eating disorders and those with psychological disorders such as PHOBIAS and OBSESSIVE-COMPULSIVE DISORDER.

Treatment for Eating Disorders

The first and most important component for treatment of eating disorders is for the person to admit that she has one.

How Can I Avoid an Eating Disorder?

Many teens refuse to believe that they are in danger and consequently won't own up to the problem.

Once a person comes to terms with the fact that she has an eating disorder, treatment can begin. Treatment for anorexia nervosa starts with a thorough medical examination to look for the presence of complications such as dehydration, irregular heart function, and abnormal blood values of electrolytes (such as potassium). Sometimes, immediate hospitalization is necessary for individuals suffering from severe dehydration or other physical complications.

Nutritional rehabilitation is necessary for treatment to be a success, and this can be very hard for young people who have an AVERSION to eating. Therefore, psychotherapy plays a crucial role in treatment. Together with the therapist, the teen suffering from anorexia nervosa will focus on self-image and distorted perceptions of body image and size.

Treatment for bulimia nervosa also begins with a thorough medical examination to look for medical complications, and the person suffering from it may be hospitalized. Again, psychotherapy plays a critical function in the treatment of bulimia. The therapy for both anorexia and bulimia often does not focus on the actual eating behaviors, but the causes behind those behaviors. Family members must be involved in therapy, too, since they often unwittingly reinforced the teen's quest for thinness or contributed to the teen's attitude toward food and eating.

Binge eating requires a different approach, for it often results in a person being overweight rather than underweight. Again, the first step for someone who binge eats is to admit that they have a problem. It's important to know that this is a common problem in North America and many people suffer from it. Talking with a trusted doctor, parent, or friend is a good first step.

Individuals with eating disorders may diet or exercise compulsively, convinced they are too heavy even when they are actually thin.

How Can I Avoid an Eating Disorder?

A doctor or psychologist can talk to you about your eating disorder.

Weight Management

Binge eaters are often tempted to go on crash diets or other extreme forms of losing weight quickly. However, as we've seen throughout the book, these types of diets are unhealthy and potentially dangerous. Plus, they don't work. Someone with a binge eating disorder should see a doctor for a complete medical exam. The doctor will then explain to the person how best to lose weight. Remember, each person's body type, size, and amount of extra weight will determine the exercise program and diet outlined by the person's physician.

Psychologists and other therapists can also help with the emotional aspects related to food, dieting, and eating. Nutritionists or dietitians can help people learn about healthy eating behaviors. They can also help teens develop a sensible eating plan for life.

It's best to keep in mind that treatment for all three eating disorders will take some time and lots of patience. Unlike problems associated with drugs, alcohol, or cigarettes, which are usually best to avoid altogether, no one can avoid eating. It can take a lot of therapy to learn healthy eating behaviors.

How to Avoid an Eating Disorder

Unfortunately, many health experts realize that prevention of eating disorders is often not possible. The best defense is to have a realistic, healthy attitude toward food, weight, and dieting. Teens who think they have an eating disorder or know someone who does can seek help from a parent, teacher, friend, or health care professional.

8

How Do I Achieve
a Healthy Lifestyle?

Six months after Jenny changed her eating habits and increased her level of physical activity, she was down almost 20 pounds and well on her way to achieving her ideal weight.

She still occasionally eats foods like cake and ice cream, but she takes a smaller portion than she used to. She also eats a lot more fresh vegetables to help offset any high-Calorie/high-fat food.

Jenny's success comes from the fact that she changed her relationship with food. She realized that she often ate out of boredom. Now, if she gets bored, she takes her dog for a walk, or rides her bike around the neighborhood. When the winter arrives in Jenny's area, she plans on using the treadmill at her gym so she can keep walking, even if it's freezing outside.

Losing Weight and Keeping it Off

Many people who are overweight or obese like Jenny decide not to diet per se. Instead they concentrate on choosing lower

Teens need to find interesting activities—rather than turning to food when they are bored.

Weight Management

fat, healthier foods and engaging more frequently in physical activity.

Weight loss does take time. Losing weight by following the dietary guidelines in MyPlate for a balanced diet and combining them with regular exercise helps to keep a steady weight once a person reaches his or her ideal weight.

The most important thing to remember is that following the dietary guidelines is not a temporary strategy but a life-long change. That is why it is not considered a diet. People who lose weight quickly and then go back to their previous eating habits before the "diet" tend to gain most, if not all, of the weight back. People who habitually diet will probably find that they gain back more weight than before. This pattern is unhealthy for a person's body and can lead to poor self-esteem for anyone who keeps losing and gaining weight.

The most sensible thing for an overweight or obese person to do is to change their ideas about food. Food is there to nourish us and keep us healthy, not to comfort us or keep us entertained when we are bored. Knowing how to eat well takes a life-long commitment to changing eating and exercise habits. Success comes from making changes that one can comfortably live with. Fortunately, teens are in a great place to make these lifelong changes because they are on the verge of moving out on their own and becoming responsible for their own food purchases, daily schedule, and lifestyle habits. It's a wonderful time to start making the necessary changes that will benefit a teen's health for life.

Assessing Your Diet

So how does a person really start to change their eating habits? For starters, it's good to keep a food diary for a few days to evaluate how much you eat and why. This will help you discover

what and how much you really eat, and whether you eat for reasons other than hunger. A food diary also helps a person keep track of food they might otherwise overlook—for example, that half bag of potato chips scarfed down while absentmindedly watching television, or those two candy bars eaten quickly after school.

To do this, for three days carry a small notebook around with you and write down everything you eat right when you eat it. Note the circumstances (lunch at school or snack at work, etc.) and exactly what and how much you eat. Also note the reasons for eating, such as "hunger," "boredom," or "loneliness." Be specific! These measures are important for people trying to lose weight. As accurately as possible, also write down the serving size for each piece of food that crosses your lips (you won't have to do this always; this diary is just to give you an idea of where you can make changes). For example, if you eat a ham sandwich, write down the details—three slices of ham, two slices of wheat bread, one tablespoon mayonnaise, one slice iceberg lettuce, one slice tomato.

Follow these steps for three days. They don't have to be consecutive days, but it's good to include two weekdays and one weekend day. Choose twenty-four-hour periods that most clearly and accurately reflect your usual dietary pattern. Carry the diary with you at all times during this period, so that you can immediately write down the foods and beverages as you consume them.

Be as specific as possible. Write down brand names of the products (for example Coke, twelve ounces), and all the ingredients in or on what you eat. Include any toppings (for example maple syrup or chocolate sauce) and how the food was prepared (baked, broiled, fried, steamed, deep-fried, etc.). Write down if the food was canned, fresh, frozen, or processed, and include

Weight Management

Keeping a food journal is a good diet strategy.

How Do I Achieve a Healthy Lifestyle?

the type of liquid in which it was packed (heavy syrup, water, juice, etc.). If possible, keep track of the food labels from these products, and write down the measurements in your diary.

After the three days are over, analyze which foods are highest in fat. Tally up a day's worth of total Calories, protein, vitamins, minerals, and fats. Next, analyze the diary to identify any of these patterns:

· eating when you aren't hungry
· skipping meals
· eating between meals
· eating in response to stress or mood swings
· overeating
· undereating
· eating the same foods all the time

With the assistance of a doctor, nutritionist, or dietitian, you can figure out the best way to make changes in your eating habits to make healthier food choices. And remember, the diary is useful in the beginning to analyze your diet. But you should not become too obsessive about every Calorie that enters your mouth. Just use this information to create a healthy eating plan and to identify trouble spots, then set it aside and focus on the necessary changes.

Changing Eating Habits

After you've analyzed your eating habits, these five simple steps can help you change the way you eat.

Eat less saturated fat. Cut way back on fatty meats like hamburger, sausage, bacon and cold cuts, all fried foods, butter, whole milk, full-fat cheeses, ice cream, salad dressing and mayo, and rich sauces and desserts. Instead choose these: lean

beef, chicken, and fish, veggie burgers, low-fat dairy products, mustard instead of mayo, and fruit or fruit popsicles for dessert. Cook foods by baking, broiling, and steaming instead of frying.

Reduce portion sizes. Forget super-sizing or "biggie-sized" meals. Even muffins, cakes, pizzas, and movie theater popcorn now come in huge portions. The simplest way to start is to cut all the portions in half. At home, use smaller plates. Eat one piece of chicken instead of two, half of a baked potato instead of a whole one, etc. When eating out, order the smallest size or share with a friend, or take half the meal home for lunch the next day.

Stop eating when you are full. All too often, people keep eating simply because there's food on their plates. How often have we heard our parents or grandparents reprimand us, "Finish what's on your plate!" This is the time to gently remind our parents that we are full and would like to be excused.

Snack on fresh fruits and vegetables. MyPlate recommends seven to nine servings of fruits and vegetables per day. These will fill you up with a wealth of essential nutrients, vitamins, and minerals, as well as complex carbohydrates and fiber. Try baby carrots, apples, oranges, sliced veggies, or vegetable soup. Avoid rich and greasy snacks like French fries, nachos, candy bars, and cookies. Avoid the vending machines, and pack your own snacks instead.

Drink water instead of soda and soft drinks. The average teen drinks three cans of soda per day. Just by eliminating the sodas, a teen could lose a pound per week. Soda is just empty Calories, heavily sweetened sugar water with about 160 Calories per can. Water, on the other hand, flushes out toxins and waste products and aids in weight loss— all with no Calories. We need to drink several glasses of water every day.

Going to a gym on a regular basis is a good way to make sure you get enough excercise to stay healthy.

Weight Management

Increasing Physical Activity

Teens who are trying to lose weight can still eat some of the higher-fat foods mentioned above; the trick is to eat them in moderation and to get regular physical activity. Virtually every study performed on people who have successfully lost weight and kept it off were people who had become aerobically active and exercised regularly.

A simple start to getting more exercise is to take the stairs instead of the escalator or elevator, walk or bike to school, and turn off the television to walk the dog, rollerblade, swim, or do anything that gets you outside and moving. Eventually, as outlined in chapter 6, the goal is to get to a point where you are exercising aerobically for about 45 minutes a few times per week. Check with your doctor if you want to do more.

Long-Term Goals: A Realistic Approach

Healthy weight management is all about being at a weight that is right for you. As discussed in the first chapter, this depends on your height, body type, gender, and level of activity. Once you've acquired a weight that is healthy and right for you, successful weight management depends on regular exercise and eating a balanced diet.

The good news is that once someone changes their attitude toward food and invests time and energy into eating well and exercising regularly, it starts to feel "natural." Health improves, attitudes improve, self-image improves. Best of all, however, is the knowledge that you can succeed and manage your weight for the rest of your life simply by participating in fun and active activities and by learning to love all kinds of delicious, healthy foods. In the long run, you may come to realize that you are not denying yourself anything so much as providing your body with what it truly needs.

Further Reading

Favor, Lesli J. and Elizabeth Massie. *Weighing In: Nutrition and Weight Management*. New York: Benchmark Books, 2009.

Jasper, Maura and Hilken Mancini. *Punk Rock Aerobics*. New York: DaCapo Press, 2004.

Levy, Lance, M.D. *Understanding Obesity*. Buffalo, N.Y.: Firefly Books, 2000.

Pitman, Teresa and Miriam Kaufman, M.D. *The Overweight Child*. Buffalo, N.Y.: Firefly Books, 2000.

Smolin, Lori A. and Mary B. Grosvenor. *Nutrition and Weight Management*. London: Chelsea House Publishers, 2010.

For More Information

Academy of Nutrition and Dietetics
www.eatright.org

Obesity Society
www.obesity.org

Blubber Busters (a website for teens and pre-teens and their parents):
www.blubberbuster.com/index.html

National Weight Control Registry
www.nwcr.ws

Overweight Children and Adolescents
www.surgeongeneral.gov/topics/obesity/calltoaction/fact_
    adolescents.htm

Punk Rock Aerobics
www.punkrockaerobics.com/index1.html

Teens' Health
www.kidshealth.org/teen

United States Food and Drug Administration
www.fda.gov

Weight Control Information Network (WIN)
www.win.niddk.nih.gov/index.htm

Publisher's note:
The websites listed on these pages were active at the time of publication. The publisher is not responsible for websites that have changed their addresses or discontinued operation since the date of publication. The publisher will review and update the websites upon each reprint.

Glossary

AEROBIC EXERCISES Sustained vigorous exercise that enhances circulation and respiratory efficiency.

ARRHYTHMIA An irregular heartbeat.

ATROPHY To decrease in size or waste away.

AVERSION An intense dislike for.

CHASTISED Punished or criticized severely.

COMPULSION An irresistible impulse to do something.

CURED A meat-processing method involving chemicals such as salt.

DEHYDRATION The condition in which the body is extremely lacking fluids.

DIETITIANS Professional who specialize in the science of nutrition and diets.

EDEMA An abnormal swelling, often in the hands and feet.

EFFICACY The ability to produce a result, usually efficiently and in a positive form.

ELECTROLYTE An ion required by cells to regulate the electrical charge and flow of water molecules across the cell membrane.

ESOPHAGUS The muscular tube that carries swallowed foods from the throat to the stomach.

GENETIC Relating to heredity.

HEMORRHOIDS A mass of veins and swollen tissues near the rectum.

INHERENT A characteristic of something that comes from nature or habit.

LETHARGY Unusual sluggishness, drowsiness.

METABOLISM The chemical changes in living cells by which energy is provided for vital processes and activities.

NUTRITIONISTS Specialists in the study of how the body uses food substances.

OBSESSIVE-COMPULSIVE DISORDER A personality disorder characterized by a preoccupation with perfectionism, need for control, and orderliness.

OPTIMUM The most favorable degree of something.

OSTEOPOROSIS A condition that is characterized by loss of bone mass, affecting primarily older women.

PALATABLE Agreeable taste.

PHOBIAS Exaggerated fears.

PLAQUE A deposit of fatty material that can form on the lining of artery walls.

PREJUDICE A negative opinion of someone or something, often based on race or ethnic background, without sufficient grounds or with incorrect knowledge.

SEIZURES A sudden attack of spasms and convulsions as in epilepsy.

STEREOTYPE An oversimplified opinion of someone, or group, based on prejudiced attitude or uncritical judgment.

TYPE II DIABETES A form of diabetes that most often begins in adulthood, characterized by inadequate secretion of insulation to sustain normal metabolism; often caused by obesity.

Index

Picture Credits

Andres Rodriguez | Dreamstime.com : p. 82
Artville pp. 10, 24, 52, 70, 96, 110
EyeWire pp. 27, 40, 84
Image Source p. 13
Joanne Zh | Dreamstime.com: p. 31
Masterseries p. 104
PhotoAlto pp. 98, 107, 112
Photodisc pp. 14, 17, 18, 28, 42
Photos.com pp. 22, 33, 34, 36, 38, 45, 46, 48, 50, 55, 57, 58, 61, 62, 65, 68, 73, 74, 77, 79, 82, 86, 89, 115
United States Department of Agriculture p. 21
Vania Dobrinova | Dreamstime.com: p. 118
Wavebreakmedia Ltd | Dreamstime.com: p. 108

The individuals in these images are models, and the images are for illustrative purposes only.

To the best knowledge of the publisher, all other images are in the public domain. If any image has been inadvertantly un-credited or miscredited, please notify Vestal Creative Services, Vestal, New York, 13850, so that rectification can be made for future printings.

Biographies

Elizabeth Bauchner lives in Ithaca, New York. A lifelong "health nut," Elizabeth enjoys bicycling, hiking and swimming with her children. She writes about healthy vegetarian food and nutrition for ChefMom.com, as well as the *Ithaca Journal*. She's also written many articles on women's and children's health issues for consumer and trade publications.

Mary Ann McDonnell, Ph.D., R.N., is the owner of South Shore Psychiatric Services, where she provides psychiatric services to children and adolescents. She has worked as a psychiatric nurse at Franciscan Hospital for Children and has been a clinical instructor for Northeastern University and Boston College advanced-practice nursing students. She was also the director of clinical trials in the pediatric psychopharmacology research unit at Massachusetts General Hospital. Her areas of expertise are bipolar disorder in children and adolescents, ADHD, and depression.

Dr. Sara Forman is a board certified physician in Adolescent Medicine. She has worked at Bentley Student Health Services since 1995 as a Senior Consulting Physician. Dr. Forman graduated from Barnard College and Harvard Medical School and completed her residency in Pediatrics at Children's Hospital of Philadelphia. After completing a fellowship in Adolescent Medicine at Children's Hospital Boston (CHB), she became an attending physician in that division. Dr. Forman's specialties include general adolescent health and eating disorders. She is the Director of the Outpatient Eating Disorders Program at Children's Hospital in Boston. In addition to seeing students at Bentley College, Dr. Forman sees primary care adolescent patients in the Adolescent Clinic at Children's and at The Germaine Lawrence School, a residential school for emotionally disturbed teenage girls.